SOLOS

for the

HORN

PLAYER

With Piano Accompaniment

Selected and Edited by

MASON JONES

ED 2462

ISBN 978-0-7935-5400-3

G. SCHIRMER, Inc.

DISTRIBUTED BY

HAL•LEONARD®
CORPORATION

7777 W. BLUEMOUND RD. P.O. BOX 13819 MILWAUKEE, WI 53213

Note

This collection of French horn music offers a variety of solos for the horn player. Its material ranges from the seventeenth century *Kirchen Arie* of Stradella to the contemporary *Largo and Allegro* by Frackenpohl.

A great deal of French horn music is written to bring out the romantic and lyric nature of the instrument. While music of this type is included here, I have added some *Scherzi* of Beethoven and Brahms, who utilized so effectively the fanfare-like aspect of the horn.

Old friends such as Glazunov and Dukas are present as well as some new ones — Lefebvre and Labor.

Each composer selected has an original, personal gift in writing for the instrument, but whether the music is slow and contemplative or brash and shouting, the poetry of the horn is always evident. This gamut of expression is latent in this collection and is ready to be recreated by the player.

I wish to thank Mr. Vlamir Sokoloff for his valuable assistance in preparing some of the piano parts.

Mason Jones

CONTENTS

		Piano	Horn
ANDANTE (from: *Symphony No. 5, "Reformation"*)	Felix Mendelssohn	28	12
ARIA (*Kirchen Arie*)	Alessandro Stradella	1	4
I ATTEMPT FROM LOVE'S SICKNESS TO FLY	Henry Purcell	5	5
I SEE A HUNTSMAN (from: *Julius Caesar*)	George Frideric Handel	9	6
LARGO AND ALLEGRO	Arthur Frackenpohl	87	29
PAVANE POUR UNE INFANTE DÉFUNTE	Maurice Ravel	81	28
REVERIES	Alexander Glazunov	61	22
ROMANCE	Charles Lefebvre	53	20
ROMANCE	Camille Saint-Saëns	35	14
RONDO (from: *Horn Quintet, K. 407*)	Wolfgang Amadeus Mozart	14	7
SCHERZO (from: *Septet, Op. 20*)	Ludwig van Beethoven	23	10
SCHERZO (from: *Serenade in D, Op. 11*)	Johannes Brahms	31	13
THEME AND VARIATIONS	Joseph Labor	39	16
VILLANELLE	Paul Dukas	65	23

Index by Composers

		Piano	Horn
LUDWIG VAN BEETHOVEN	Scherzo (from: *Septet, Op. 20*)	23	10
JOHANNES BRAHMS	Scherzo (from: *Serenade in D, Op. 11*)	31	13
PAUL DUKAS	Villanelle	65	23
ARTHUR FRACKENPOHL	Largo and Allegro	87	29
ALEXANDER GLAZUNOV	Reveries	61	22
GEORGE FRIDERIC HANDEL	I See a Huntsman (from: *Julius Caesar*)	9	6
JOSEPH LABOR	Theme and Variations	39	16
CHARLES LEFEBVRE	Romance	53	20
FELIX MENDELSSOHN	Andante (from: *Symphony No. 5, "Reformation"*)	28	12
WOLFGANG AMADEUS MOZART	Rondo (from: *Horn Quintet, K. 407*)	14	7
HENRY PURCELL	I Attempt from Love's Sickness to Fly	5	5
MAURICE RAVEL	Pavane pour une Infante défunte	81	28
CAMILLE SAINT-SAËNS	Romance	35	14
ALESSANDRO STRADELLA	Aria (*Kirchen Arie*)	1	4

1. Aria

(Kirchen Arie)

1667

ALESSANDRO STRADELLA (1642-1682)
Arranged by M.J.

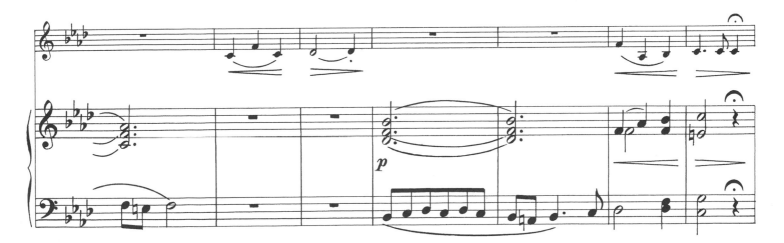

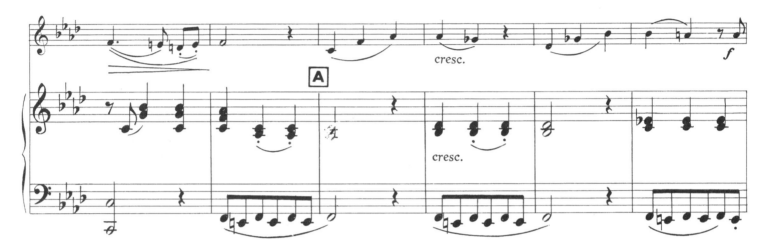

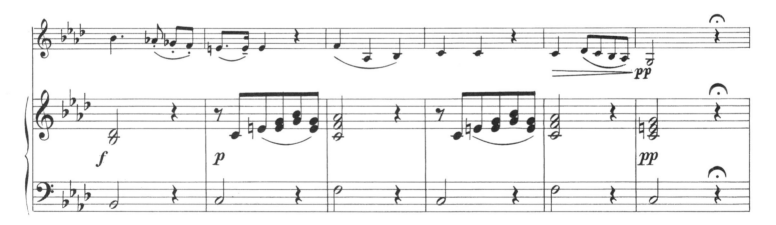

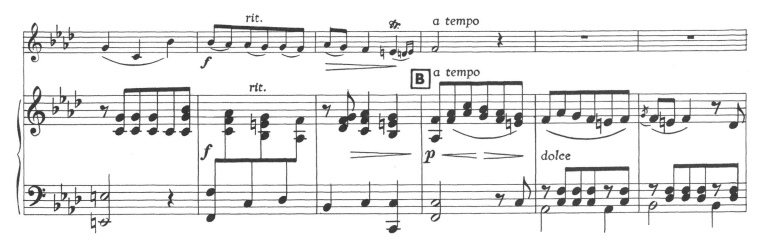

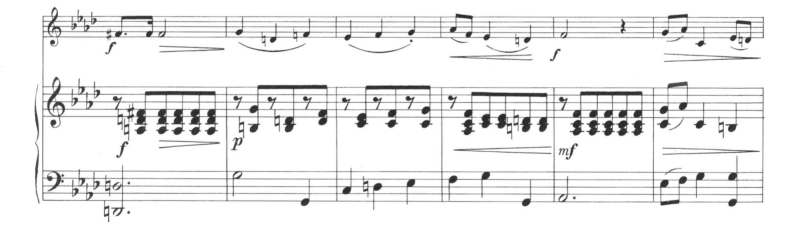

2. I Attempt from Love's Sickness to Fly

HENRY PURCELL (c. 1659-1695)
Arranged by M.J.

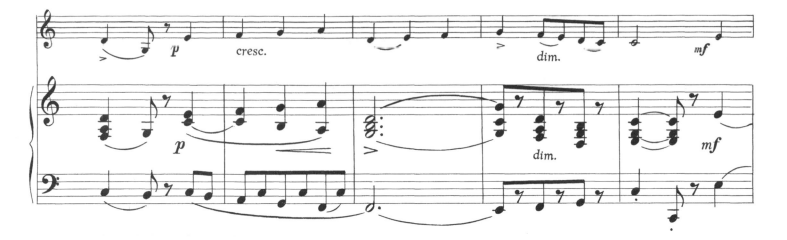

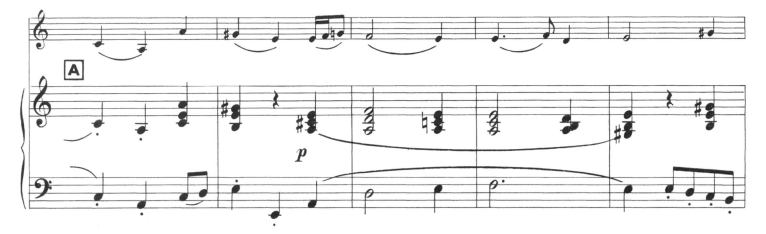

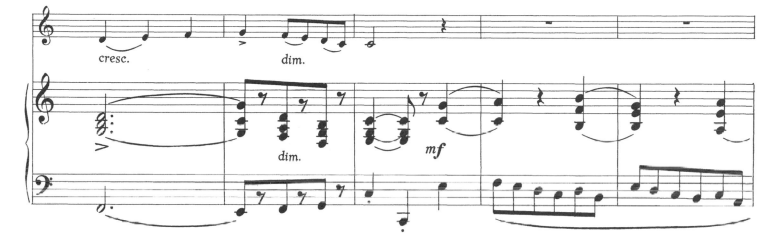

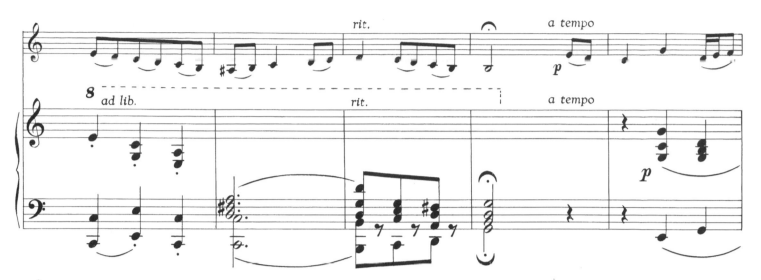

3. I See a Huntsman

from: Julius Caesar

GEORGE FRIDERIC HANDEL (1685-1759)
Arranged by M.J.

13

4. Rondo

from: Horn Quintet, K.407

WOLFGANG AMADEUS MOZART (1756-1791)
Arranged by M.J.

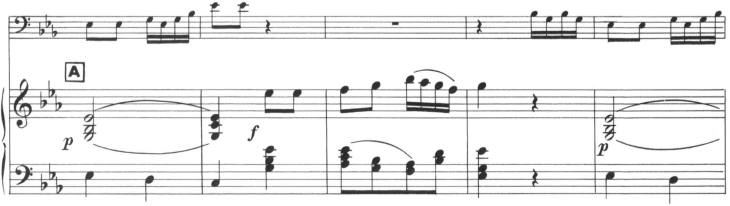

15

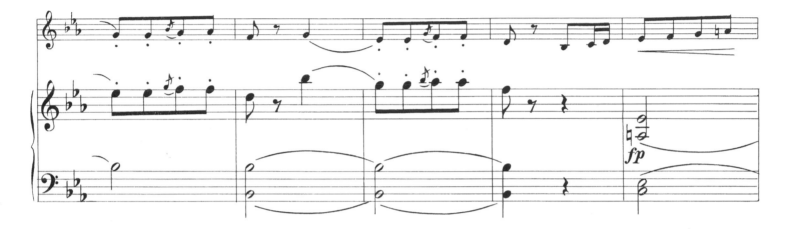

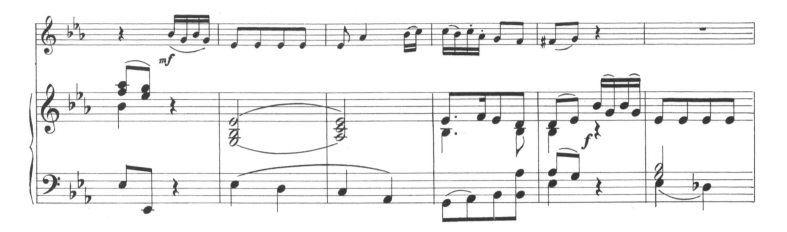

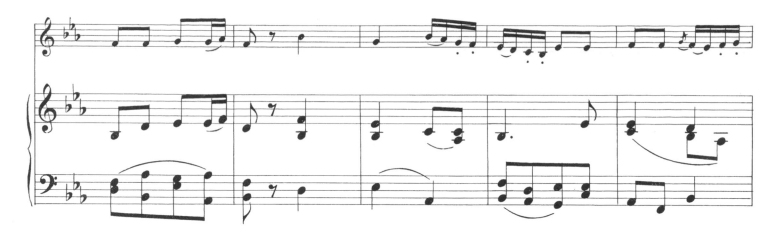

21

5. Scherzo

from: Septet, Op. 20

LUDWIG VAN BEETHOVEN (1770-1827)
Arranged by M.J.

Allegro molto e vivace

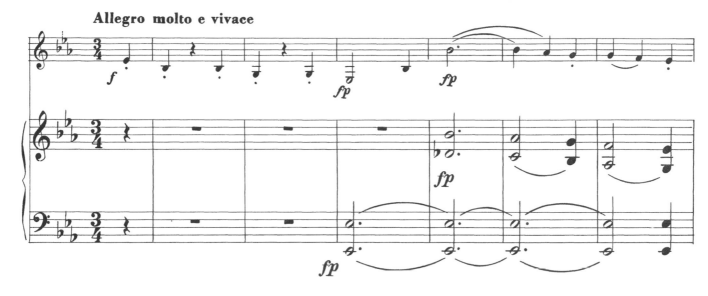

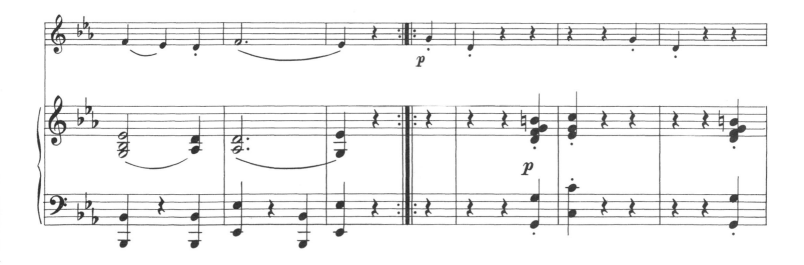

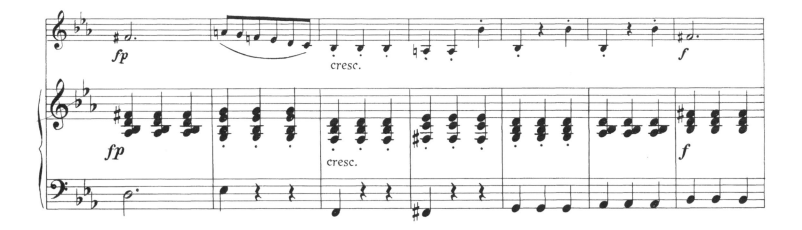

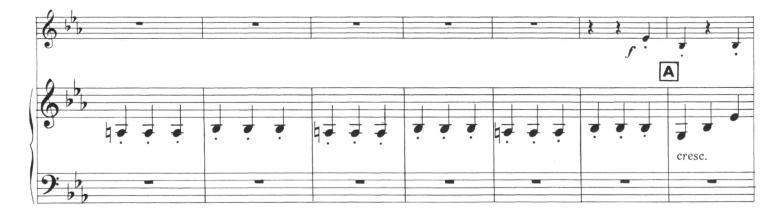

26

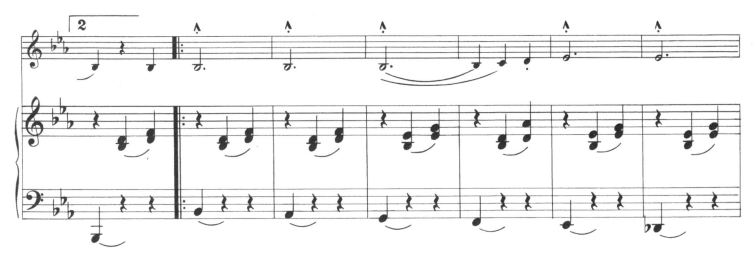

6. Andante

from: Symphony No. 5, "Reformation"

FELIX MENDELSSOHN (1809-1847)
Arranged by M.J.

7. Scherzo

from: Serenade in D, Op. 11

JOHANNES BRAHMS, (1833-1897)
Arranged by M.J.

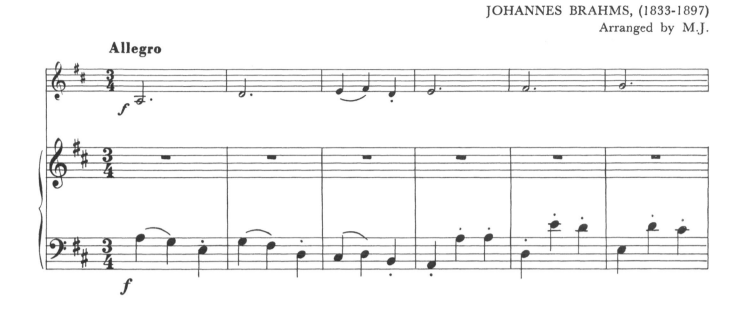

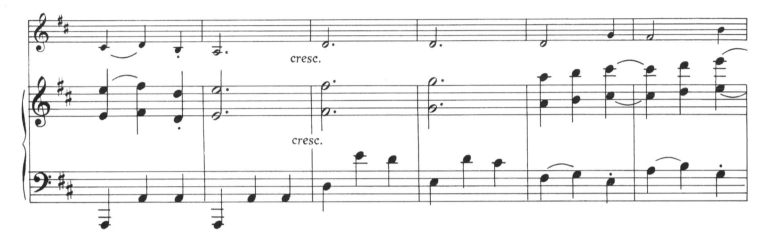

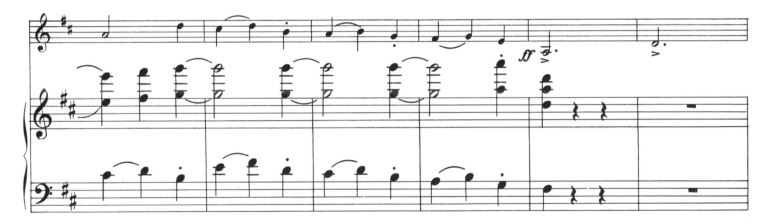

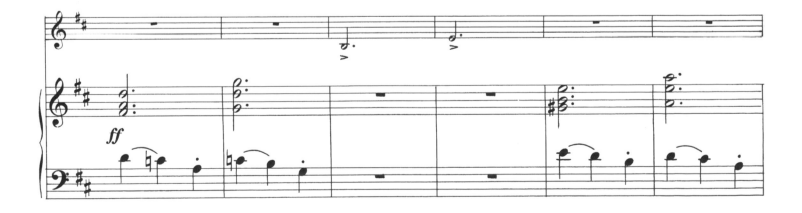

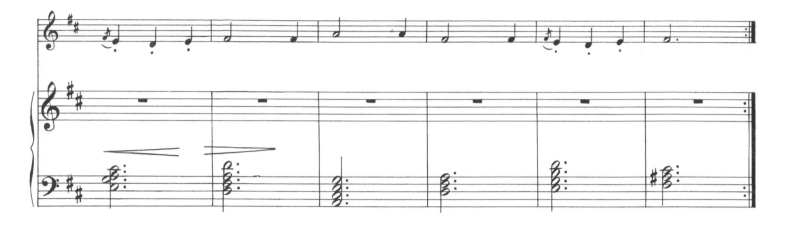

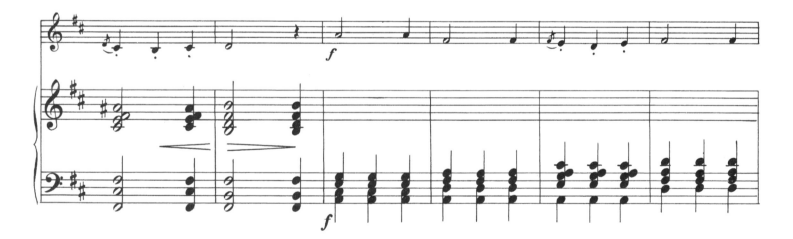

8. Romance

CAMILLE SAINT-SAËNS, Op. 36
(1835-1921)

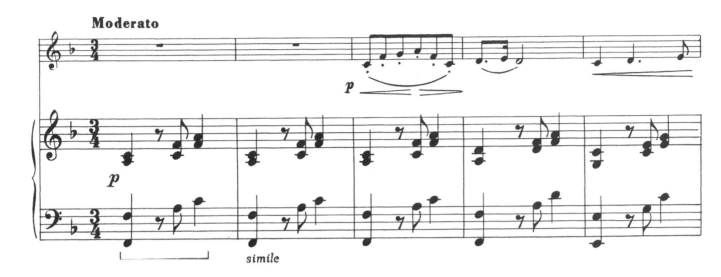

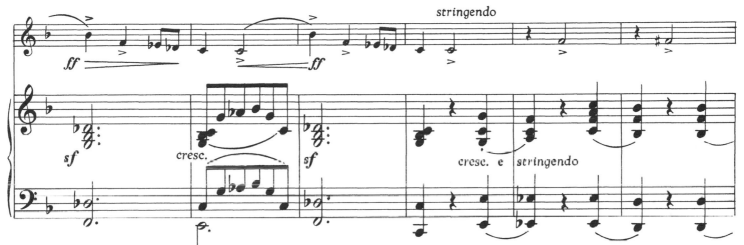

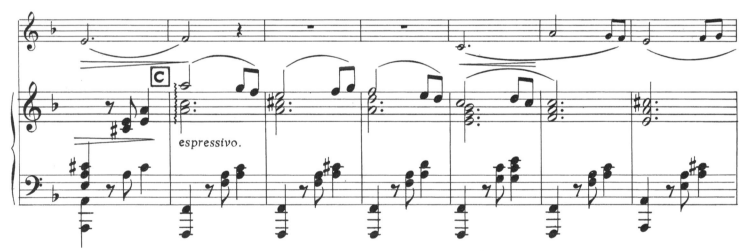

9. Theme and Variations

JOSEPH LABOR, Op. 10
(1842-1924)

Theme
Andantino

Var. I

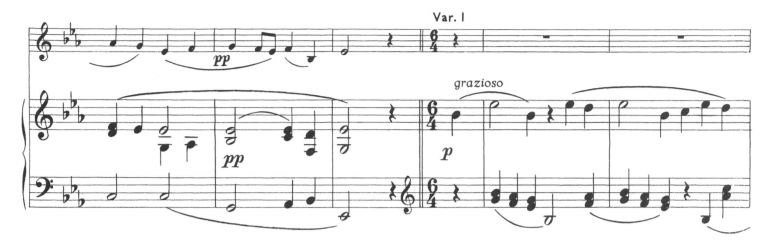

Var. II
Allegro

Var. III
Andante

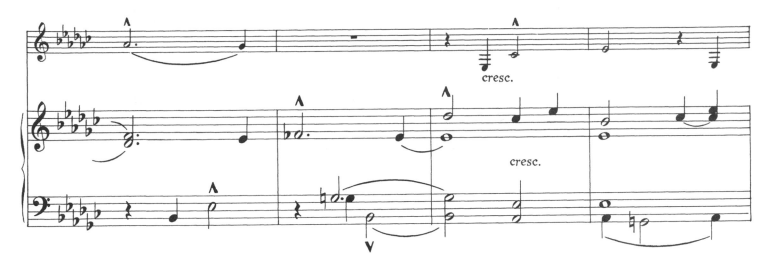

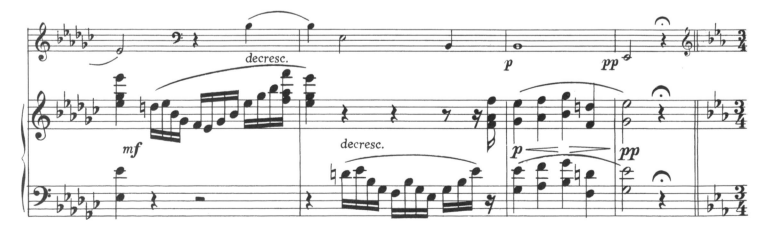

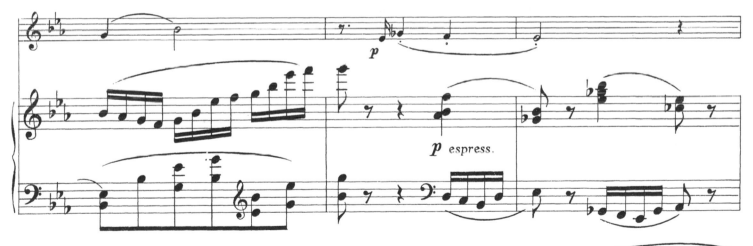

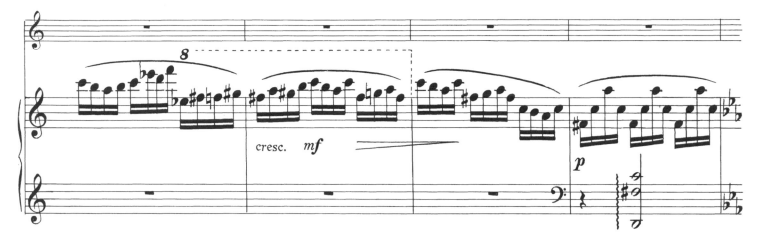

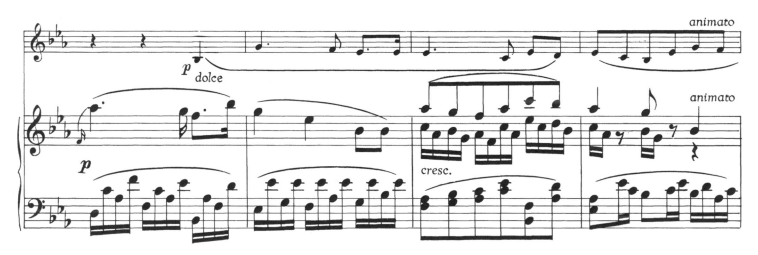

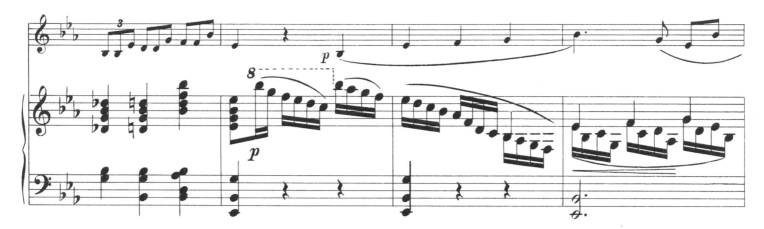

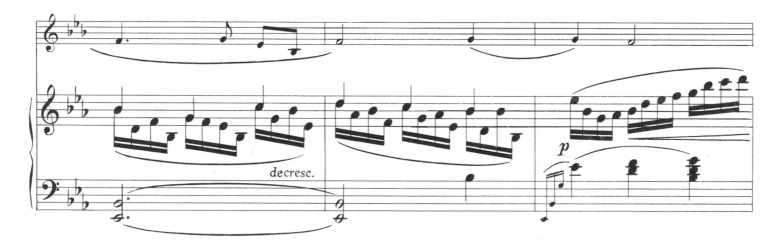

10. Romance

CHARLES LEFEBVRE, Op. 30
(1843-1917)

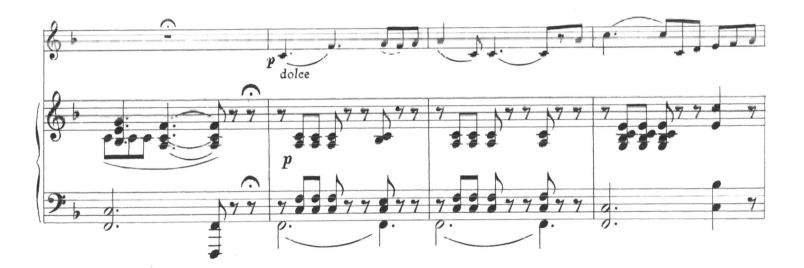

poco a poco cresc.

poco a poco cresc.

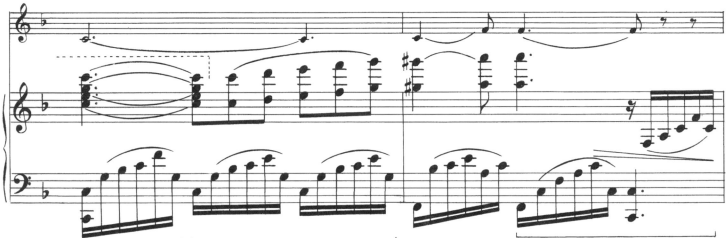

11. Reveries

ALEXANDER GLAZUNOV, Op. 24
(1865-1936)

12. Villanelle

PAUL DUKAS (1865-1935)

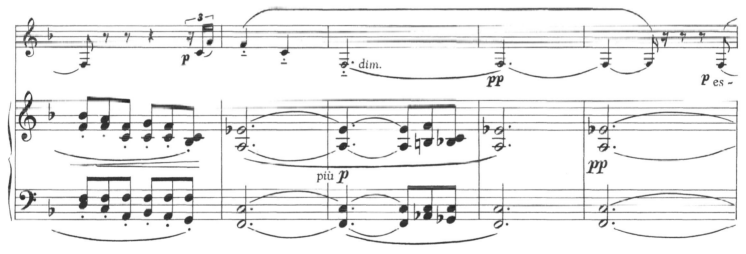

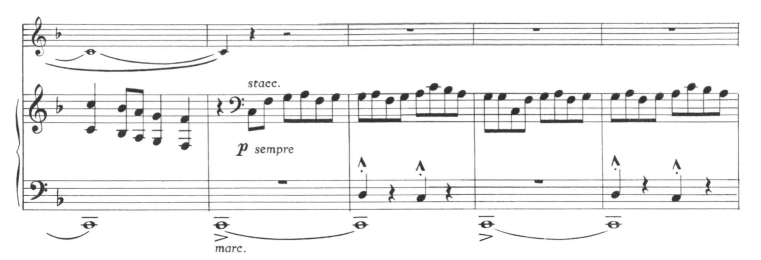

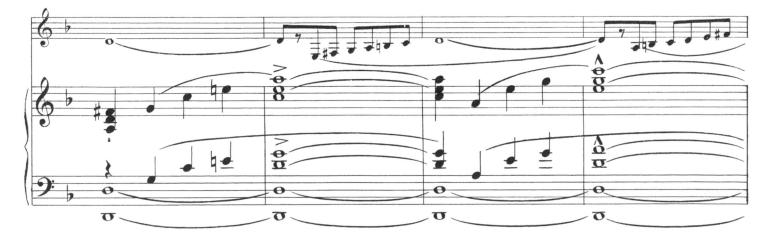

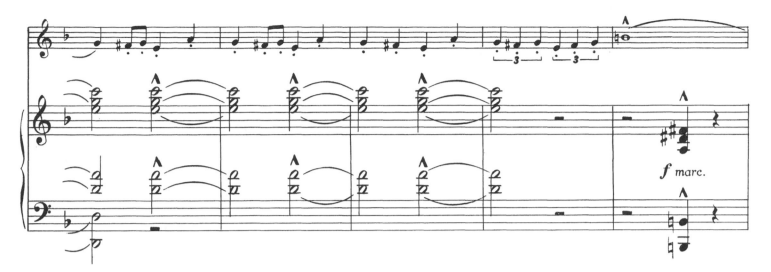

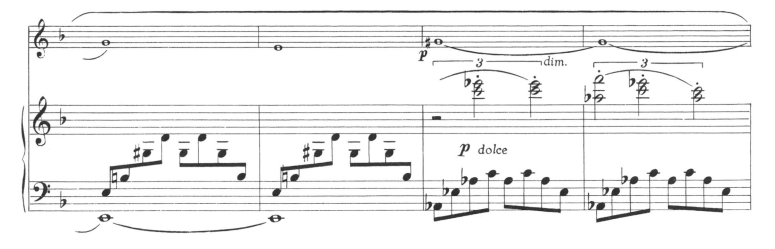

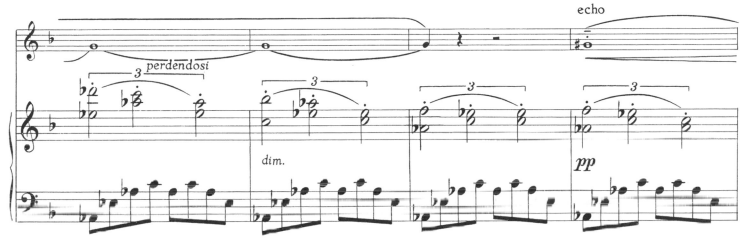

Légèrement retenu *(slightly slower)*

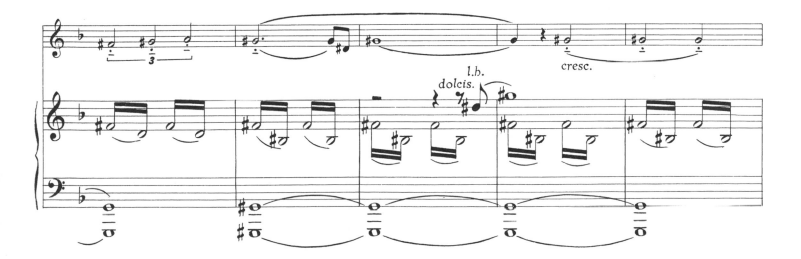

dim.

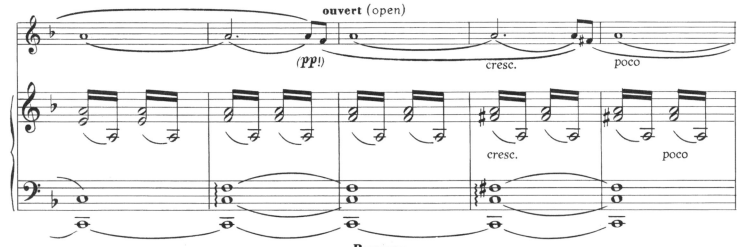

ouvert (open)

(pp!)   cresc.   poco

cresc.   poco

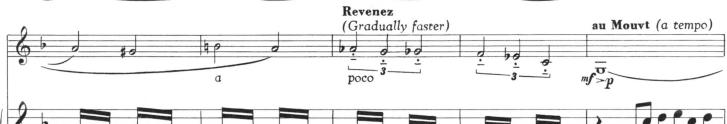

Revenez
(Gradually faster)   **au Mouvt** (a tempo)

a   poco   mf > p

a   poco   mf p stacc. leggiero

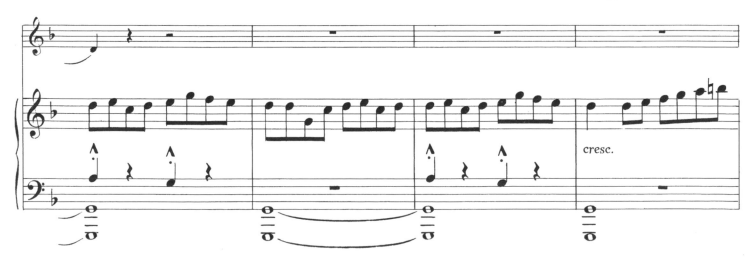

cresc.

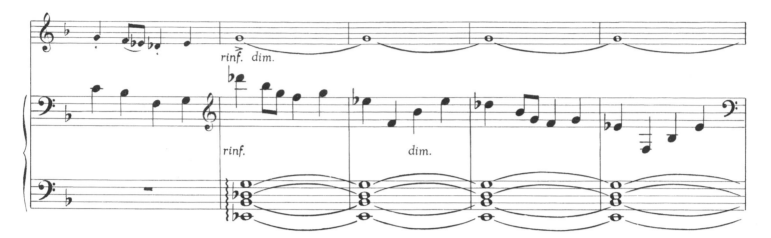

poco rit.

a tempo
avec sourdine (muted)

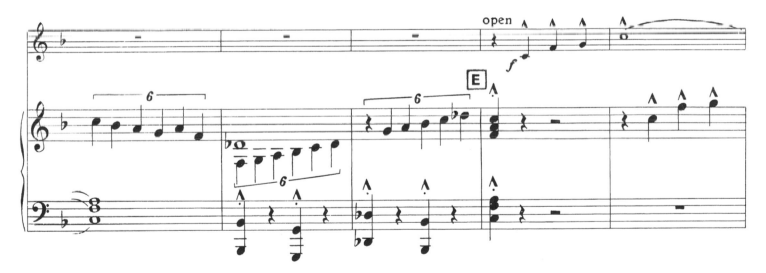

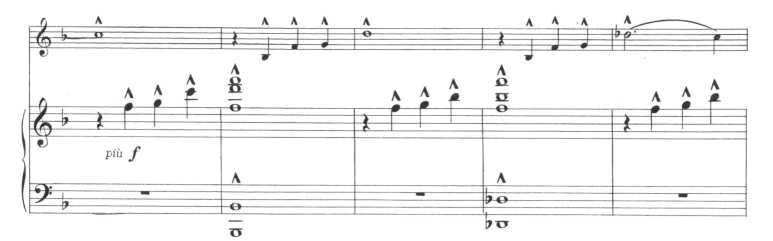

Retenez beaucoup (*molto rit.*)

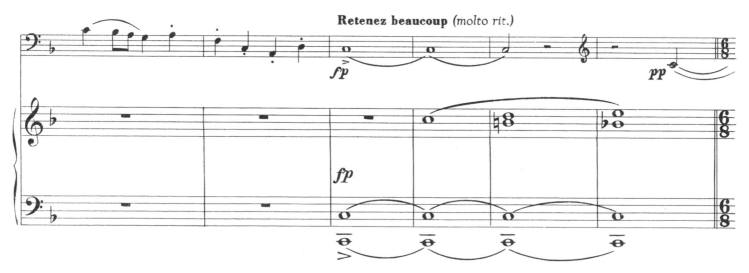

13. Pavane pour une Infante défunte

MAURICE RAVEL (1875-1937)
Arranged by M.J.

Assez doux, mais d'une sonorité large
(Rather gently, but with a broad sonority)

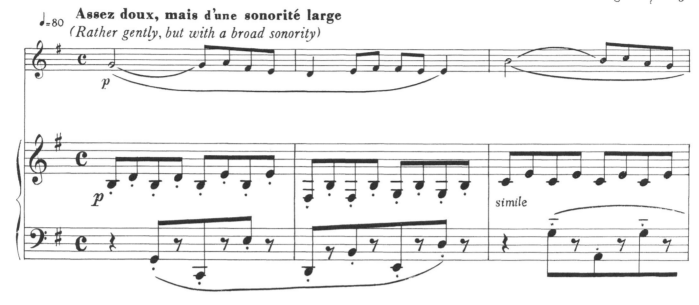

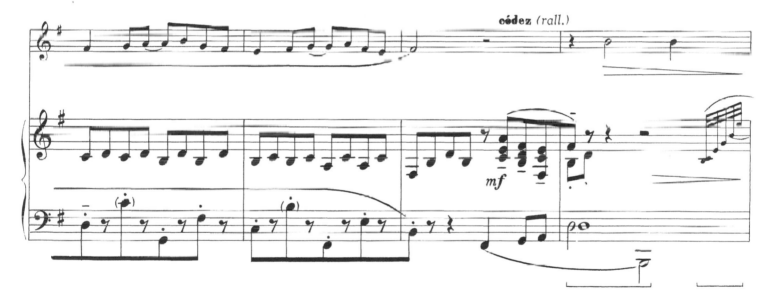

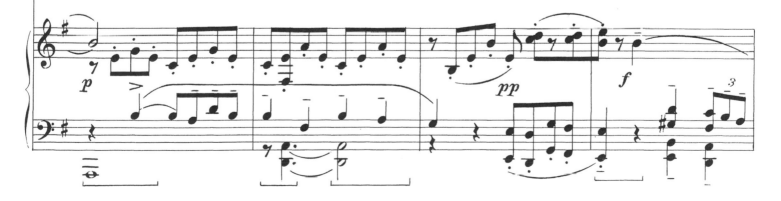

Très lointain (*very distant*)
1er Mouvement (*Tempo I*)

Très soutenu (*very sustained*)

un peu plus lent *(slightly slower)*

Reprenez le mouvement *(a tempo)*

A

simile

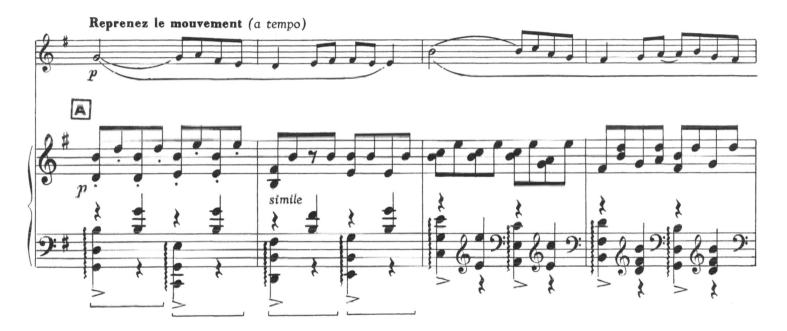

cédez *(rall.)*

en mesure (*a tempo*)

large (*broadly*)

1er Mouvement (*Tempo I*)

B

subitement très doux et très lié
(*suddenly very gentle and very sustained*)

Très grave (very solemnly)

1er Mouvement (*Tempo I*)

cédez *(rall.)*

Reprenez le mouvement *(a tempo)*

en élargissant beaucoup *(very broadly)*

14. Largo and Allegro

I

ARTHUR FRACKENPOHL (1924-   )

Note: A version of this work for horn and string orchestra, or horn and string quartet, is available on rental from G. Schirmer, Inc.

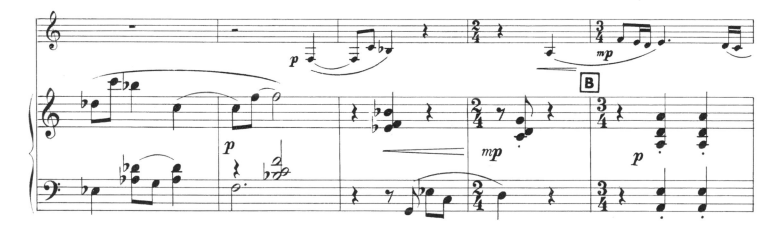

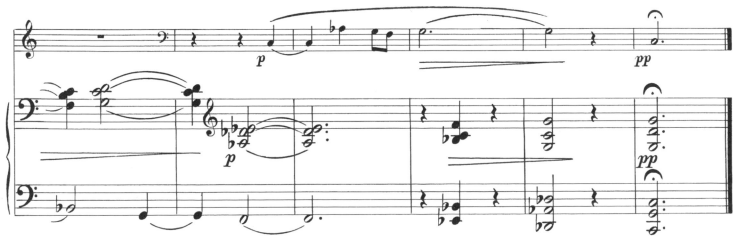

II

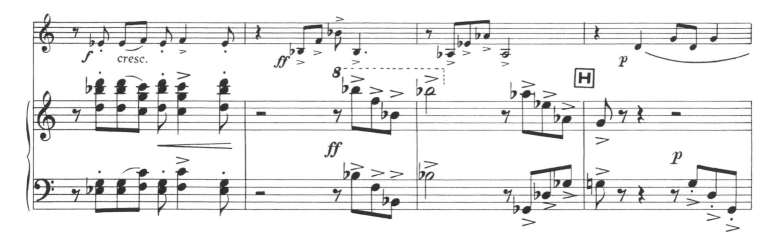

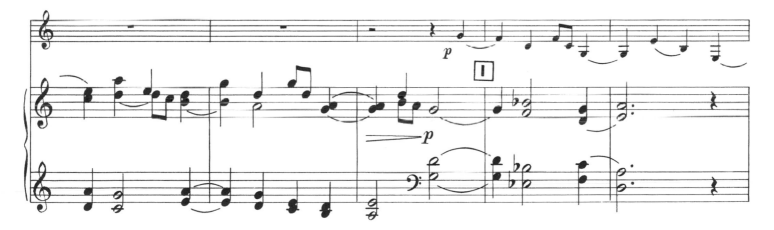

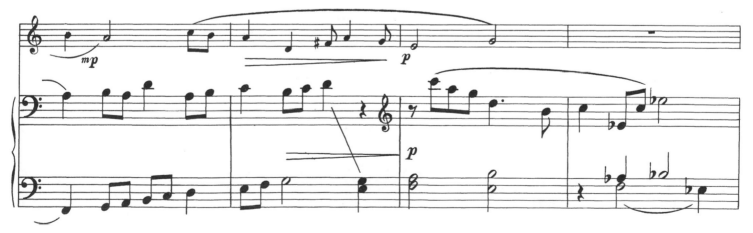